Confirmation

R E C O R D

Child's Name

Parents

Sponsor

Date of Confirmation

Bishop or Priest

Church

Address

City, State

Your Child's Confirmation

Carol Luebering

Liguori

Nihil Obstat
Rev. Lawrence Landini, O.F.M.
Rev. Edward J. Gratsch

Imprimi Potest
Rev. Fred Link, O.F.M.
Minister Provincial

Imprimatur
+Most Rev. Carl K. Moeddel
Vicar General and Auxiliary Bishop
Archdiocese of Cincinnati
February 22, 2000

The *nihil obstat* and *imprimatur* are a declaration that a book or pamphlet is considered to be free from doctrinal or moral error. It is not implied that those who have granted the *nihil obstat* and *imprimatur* agree with the contents, opinions or statements expressed.

Cover and interior illustrations by Julie Lonneman
Cover and book design by Mary Alfieri

ISBN-10: 0-86716-345-3
ISBN-13: 978- 0-86716-345-2

Published by Liguori Publications
Liguori, Missouri 63057

Liguori Publications, a nonprofit corporation, is an apostolate of the Redemptorists. To learn more about the Redemptorists, visit Redemptorists.com.

To order, visit Liguori.org or call 800-325-9521.

Printed in the U.S.A.
21 20 19 18 17   9 8 7 6 5

Contents

Introduction

Years ago you made a promise. You renounced evil and professed belief in the faith held by the Church in the name of the baby you presented for Baptism.

Soon the bishop or his representative will ask your youngster to repeat that pledge. Then he will trace a cross on your child's forehead with oil and say, "Be sealed with the gift of the Holy Spirit."

That sacramental action has roots in the New Testament and other ancient Christian writings. At the same time, its history is complex, giving rise to the confusion which still surrounds the sacrament today. We call Confirmation a *sacrament of initiation,* but it is often celebrated years after the first sacrament of initiation, Baptism. It may precede the final stage of initiation—Eucharist—or follow long after First Communion.

Confirmation celebrates the outpouring of the Holy Spirit into believers' lives—a Spirit first conferred at Baptism. It is not primarily a sacrament of mature commitment, even though it may be offered in high school years.

Seal of Baptism

As the local community grew larger, the bishop became a distant figure. His delegates, priests, baptized. Their acts were literally *confirmed* by the bishop in a later ceremony of anointing. In time, Christians began to speak of Confirmation as the "seal" of Baptism that conferred the Holy Spirit.

How can you judge your child's readiness? How free should a youngster be to make a personal decision to be confirmed—indeed, how free can a child be from subtle pressures from teachers, classmates and, of course, parents?

Your Child's Confirmation will help you sort things through. It offers background thoughts on your experience as a parent, and quotations from Scripture, the liturgy of the sacrament and the *Catechism of the Catholic Church* to ponder, as well as questions to guide your reflection and discussion.

Acquiring Christian Identity: Confirmation and Baptism

Life begins with a shock: the first breath. Newborns react to the chill intrusion with a cry that expels it and a gasp that further expands tiny lungs. Breathing is already an unconscious act.

The human body can survive for days without water, months without food, but only for minutes without breath. CPR, the Heimlich maneuver and mouth-to-mouth resuscitation are lifesaving interventions taught in first aid courses.

Presenting your child for Baptism was a lifesaving intervention. Your recognition of evil's threat and the need to circle your infant with God's support and the support of the Christian community led you to the baptismal font. There you asked the *fullness* of life for your baby. And your child rose from the water filled with new life.

Confirmation and Baptism celebrate the same reality with a slightly different focus. Baptism celebrates the *gift* of life; Confirmation celebrates the *breath* of life—the Holy Spirit. We cannot speak of one without recalling the other (or, for that matter, without mentioning Eucharist, which *nourishes* life).

The first Christians didn't think of Baptism and Confirmation as separate. The newly baptized emerged from the waters to be anointed and welcomed to the Eucharistic table in one ceremony presided over by the leader of the local Church—the bishop. The community was small—a family gathering.

Families grow—and families change as they grow. Family celebrations also change as children grow older: Christmas centered on *receiving* Santa's bounty becomes Christmas centered on *giving* delight.

The little family of believers in Jesus grew, too. The gospel became a tradition handed down from generation to generation. Infant baptism became much more common than welcoming adults into the community.

Still Desirable Sacrament

In the medieval world, many believers never received Confirmation. Travel was difficult not only for the bishops, but also for folks who lived miles outside the towns they visited. Church law treated Confirmation as "nice, but not necessary." The baptismal breath of life and the nourishment of Eucharist sustained most believers, even though Confirmation was still seen as desirable for all and necessary for ordination.

When the Protestant Reformation leader Martin Luther's insistence that Confirmation had no biblical basis and therefore was not a sacrament challenged Catholics to rethink their beliefs, Confirmation once more became an ordinary Catholic practice. Children were baptized at birth, taught their faith, then confirmed and, finally, admitted to Eucharist in their early teens—when they were virtually adults by the standards of their society.

A century ago, family custom changed once more. Pope Pius X decreed that adolescence was very late for First Communion, and he lowered the age. The sacramental order thus changed—Baptism, then Eucharist, then Confirmation—completely severing any apparent connection between Baptism and Confirmation.

Adults and school-age children are still adopted into the faith family in one celebration of Baptism, Confirmation and Eucharist. But most Catholics are baptized in infancy and initiated gradually as they grow in faith and knowledge. Our challenge is to rediscover the relationship between Baptism and Confirmation.

When should a baptized Catholic be confirmed? As of 2002, the USCCB has decreed that in accordance with Canon 891, the Latin Rite dioceses in the United States shall confer confirmation "between the age of discretion and about sixteen years of age." In terms of years, this "age of discretion" has varied widely—from about seven up to adolescence. Each diocese still determines the decision and specific limits.

Your diocese may confirm before First Communion, at the end of grade school, or even in high school. At each age, different aspects of the sacrament seem important. The confirmation of a young child often reflects parental faith. A youngster approaching adolescence is ready to start integrating the values taught throughout childhood; and a teenager who has wrestled with faith questions is capable of making a personal commitment to God and the Church.

At any age, Confirmation remains what it has always been: the completion of Baptism, one step in the process of welcoming—initiating—new members into the community whose faith rests in Jesus Christ.

For Reflection and Discussion

- *At what age is your youngster going to be confirmed? What understanding of the sacrament do you think your child has?*

- *How old were you when you were confirmed? What understanding of the sacrament did you have?*

- *How does your child's understanding of Confirmation differ from yours when you were confirmed? How does age influence this understanding?*

- *Have you ever seen your parish community receive new adult members? What did you think of the celebration?*

The God of power and Father of our Lord
Jesus Christ has freed you from sin and
brought you to new life through water
and the Holy Spirit.

He now anoints you with the chrism of salvation,
so that, united with his people, you may
remain forever a member of Christ
who is Priest, Prophet, and King.
(*Rite of Baptism for Children*, #98)

"Repent, and be baptized every one of you in
the name of Jesus Christ so that your sins may
be forgiven; and you will receive the gift of the
Holy Spirit." (Acts 2:38)

Since Baptism, Confirmation, and Eucharist form
a unity, it follows that "the faithful are obliged to
receive this sacrament at the appropriate time,"
for without Confirmation and Eucharist, ...Christian initation remains
incomplete. (*Catechism of the Catholic Church*, #1306)

Discovering Christian Identity: Confirmation and Growth

A t the moment of birth, breath is the first concern. Only when tiny lungs work will a baby survive beyond a few minutes.

With that concern comes a need to establish an identity. Someone fastened a bracelet bearing your surname on your newborn. Within days, you provided an individual name for the birth certificate. You brought your child to the baptismal font not only for formal conferral of that name, but also to give your infant a new identity: Christian, Catholic.

Adults choose what names they want to add to their own. They marry, join a political party or a professional society, a union or a volunteer group or a particular circle of friends because those groups, those people, somehow reflect and enlarge their own sense of who they are.

A small child, on the other hand, must first grow into an identity given by others. It didn't take long for your infant to recognize his or her name. A family name is a greater hurdle. It takes more than a few months for a child to learn it, to spell it, to come to some understanding of what it means to be a Sanchez or a Shea or a Sekitei. It takes time, too, for a youngster to grasp the realities of larger identities. A sense of racial, ethnic or national belonging comes slowly, absorbed over the years from celebrations and stories.

A child born into the Church slowly discovers what it means to be Catholic from the stories and customs you share. The Christmas crèche and the crucifix on the bedroom wall, family prayer and Sunday Mass, Jesus' name on your lips and more formal religion classes—all these things and more have taught your child about being a member of God's family.

Early in life, your child realized that everything can be named, that breath can form words which express reality. As your child grew, you enriched a limited vocabulary with many words and concepts. You taught your youngster God's name and taught the meaning of divine love by your love. By word and example you shared your faith.

You were not, of course, alone in that teaching effort. You introduced your child to other people who speak belief in word and action. You brought your child to the parish for more formal instruction.

Through your efforts, your youngster has grown conscious of the God-life within her. No more is the Spirit-breath an unconscious fact of life; it can be articulated. Your youngster can tell the story of Jesus' life, death and resurrection. Your child has a sense of what it means to belong to the Church, to be a part of a people called by Jesus and formed by the Spirit.

The Church to which you brought a baby for Baptism is, of course, larger than your child's personal experience—or your own—larger than a circle of believing friends, larger than your parish community. It reaches to the far corners of the earth.

Modern communications have shrunk the world. The Church's efforts to feed starving children in distant countries, papal travels, debates between bishops and governments—all these things daily invade your living room.

Today's Confirmation candidate probably has a better sense of Christian identity than any previous generation. Your youngster is ready to stand before a representative of the larger Church—the bishop or his delegate—and say, "Yes, this is my belief. This is my Church. This is who I am."

Something Lovable

Your youngster is probably also more aware of the Church's faults than candidates of previous generations. He or she has heard adult complaints. Scandals are aired on the news and such stains as the Inquisition and the persecution of the Jews appear in history books. Yet your youngster, like you, has found something lovable about this imperfect institution.

The faith you professed for your child at Baptism is not the same faith your son or daughter will carry into adulthood. Nor should it be. For all you may shake your head and sigh, "Kids! They're all alike," you know they're not. Your Confirmation candidate is unlike any other child. The human individual is the Creator's greatest achievement—a unique person who can know and respond to God as no one else can.

For Reflection and Discussion

- *What part of who you are—family, ethnic, national and religious identity—is yours by birth? What elements of your heritage have you deliberately chosen to share with your child?*

- *What do you remember of growing into your birth identity (e.g., discovering the meaning of your family name, learning your racial, ethnic or national heritage, your family's faith)? How long did it take to accept (or reject) the identity into which you were born? Do you think your youngster has been going through the same growth process? Why?*

- *How much of who you are today is a chosen identity (your occupation, your social life, your relationships)? What part of who your child is today grows out of his or her own personal choices? How happy are you with those choices? Do you find it difficult to allow your child to make those choices?*

To the poor he proclaimed the good news
of salvation,
to prisoners, freedom
and to the sorrowful of heart, joy.

To accomplish your plan,
he gave himself up to death,
and, rising from the dead,
he destroyed death and restored life.

And that we might live no longer for ourselves
but for him who died and rose again for us,
he sent the Holy Spirit from you, Father,
as the first fruits for those who believe,
so that, bringing to perfection his work
in the world,
he might sanctify creation to the full.
(Eucharistic Prayer IV)

In him [Christ] you also, when you had heard the word of truth, the gospel of your salvation, and had believed in him, were marked with the seal of the promised Holy Spirit; this is the pledge of our inheritance toward redemption as God's own people, to the praise of his glory. (Ephesians 1:13-14)

Preparation for Confirmation should aim at leading the Christian toward a more intimate union with Christ and a more lively familiarity with the Holy Spirit.... To this end catechesis for Confirmation should strive to awaken a sense of belonging to the Church of Jesus Christ, the universal Church as well as the parish community. (*Catechism of the Catholic Church,* #1309)

Affirming Christian Identity: Confirmation and Commitment

Sooner or later, every youngster has to come to personal terms with the birthright identity. It's one thing to know the traditions of a family, a people, a Church. It's another thing to choose them.

Affirming the identity conferred at birth isn't easy. Most youngsters, psychologists say, cherish an "adoption fantasy," a belief that they were really born to others. (Adopted children idealize birth parents.) All kids at some time wish they belonged to some other family.

Adolescence imposes a new search for identity. Sooner or later a child achieves the separation and independence necessary to live as an adult.

Sometimes a heritage gets left behind, abandoned. But most often the next generation follows in the footsteps of the generations before. Even the most rebellious recover their sense of belonging and maintain warm relationships in spite of differences in viewpoint.

At the same time, few people accept their heritage without reshaping it to fit their own personality and the reality of the world they know. That's especially true with religious belief. Even theologians continue to find new ways to understand ancient truths as the world continues to change at a rapid rate.

In the midst of a changing world and a changing Church, what does it mean for a Confirmation candidate to affirm the birthright belief, to make a commitment in faith?

Commitment is a word often associated with Confirmation. When long years separate Confirmation from Baptism, it seems only reasonable to view a young person's formal repetition of the baptismal promise as a more mature faith commitment. (Many Protestant traditions perceive that as the whole meaning of Confirmation.)

But human commitment is always a signature on a blank check. The vows pronounced on a wedding day pledge love unto death. Long-married couples admit having rethought and remade that commitment many times over the years.

Your own faith commitment has been subject to similar stresses, similar changes. Every time you brushed against mystery—the wonder of birth, sorrow and loss, the frustrations of everyday life—your concept of God changed a bit and you had to choose belief all over again.

Your child set out on that same journey the day you taught the first prayer. To a very small child, God and

Santa and the Easter Bunny exist in one wonderful dream world. Your youngster has formed and discarded many images of God in a very short lifetime and, like every believer, will continue to search for an accurate sense of divine reality until the end of life. Promising faith is more a lifetime effort than a one-time action.

Life is strewn with broken promises—a fact every child learns quickly and every adult acknowledges with pain. But we keep on making and receiving promises because we believe that commitment is possible, because we believe that one promise, at least, will never be broken—God's commitment to us.

That's the view of Confirmation embedded in Church law. It makes this sacrament a prerequisite to the sacraments of commitment—Marriage and Holy Orders—if it can be received without great inconvenience. The commitments believers make are possible because we believe in a God who keeps promises.

Confirmation celebrates God's promise—as do Baptism and Eucharist, the other sacraments of initiation. God is committed to us. God has given an only Son as pledge; God has sent the Spirit, the breath of life, as free gift to those who believe the divine promise.

The smallest child quickly learns whose word can be trusted. As a child learns to know who God is and how God works, he or she can begin to affirm the heritage handed down, to promise continuing trust in One whose word has already proved trustworthy.

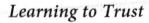

Learning to Trust

Learning to trust is the first lesson an infant learns. The assurance that someone will respond to his or her cries is essential to a baby's development. As we grow older, we also learn that sometimes the dearest people disappoint us, yet the history of care enables us to trust them again—and to become people who can also be trusted.

In Catholic tradition Confirmation is indeed a celebration of commitment—our faith in God's fidelity to us. That faith brought you to the baptismal font with an infant in your arms; you have shared it as your youngster grew. On Confirmation day, your child will be asked to repeat the creed, the Church's expression of faith in God's fidelity.

For Reflection and Discussion

- *In whom do you place your trust, and why? What has led you to put faith in the words of those people?*

- *What people and experiences have brought you to religious belief you can call your own? What has led you to trust in God's word, in the Church?*

- *What questions did you have to struggle with before you came to the faith you hold today?*

- *What questions have you watched form in your youngster's mind?*

- *Do you think your child's scrutiny of your life, your belief, has strengthened his or her own decision to follow you in faith?*

Do you believe in God, the Father almighty, creator of heaven and earth?

Do you believe in Jesus Christ, his only Son, our Lord, who was born of the Virgin Mary, was crucified, died, and was buried, rose from the dead, and is now seated at the right hand of the Father?

Do you believe in the Holy Spirit, the holy catholic Church, the communion of saints, the forgiveness of sins, the resurrection of the body, and the life everlasting? (*Rite of Baptism for Children*, #95)

In this is love, not that we loved God but that he loved us and sent his Son to be the atoning sacrifice for our sins. Beloved, since God loved us so much, we also ought to love one another. (1 John 4:10-11)

Although Confirmation is sometimes called the "sacrament of Christian maturity," we must not confuse adult faith with the adult age of natural growth, nor forget that the baptismal grace is a grace of free, unmerited election and does not need "ratification" to become effective. (*Catechism of the Catholic Church*, #1308)

Living Christian Identity: Confirmation and Witness

When your child was born, you wondered what kind of person the small stranger you welcomed would turn out to be. By now, you know. Getting acquainted has been a string of surprises. The greatest is that you can look back and trace consistency. The quick smile, the set of the jaw, the rush to speak every thought or the tendency to solitary introspection—your child's traits didn't ap-pear out of the blue. They unfolded slowly from something there from the beginning.

Looking back from Confirmation to Baptism reveals the same consistency. The Spirit, the God-breath, has been there from the beginning. But your child is much more articulate and competent. Now the soft, life-sustaining breath given at Baptism is the breath behind speech, empowering your child to raise a voice in witness.

Witness is an ancient description of the believer's role. In today's usage, it often refers to enthusiastic testimony to what the Lord has done in one's life. At the beginning of Christianity, it more often meant giving one's life. The title under which we honor the Christians who bravely faced Roman lions—*martyr*—comes from the Greek *martus*, "witness."

Through the centuries, witness has endured as a legal term for a person who speaks from personal knowledge. What a person has seen and heard remains the reality of Christian witness. Expressed in martyrdom, enthusiastic words or actions that speak concern for human needs, the Christian witness testifies to what the believer *knows*: God loves us and calls us to love. Jesus Christ personified that love and is life and hope for all the world.

The child you brought for Baptism did not know that and could not speak it. But the Spirit who inflated tiny lungs must now be more fully acknowledged, and celebrated as the impelling force in every Christian's life.

Your youngster has learned not only the Church's faith, but also how people bear witness in today's world. Your child heard you speak your belief in prayer, in the stories you told of Jesus. Your child watched as you and other significant adults in her life served the community, responding to your neighbors' needs. TV brought other forms of Christian witness into your living room: papal visits and famine relief efforts, people speaking out against injustice and for human rights. The news has reported the ultimate witness—martyrdom: missionaries slain in distant lands, hometown folks laying down their lives to save a child from an onrushing car or a burning building.

In formal religious education your youngster learned the stories of the Church's heroes, people whose lives have shouted their faith. The Confirmation program itself may have demanded service in the community as a sign of your child's readiness for the sacrament.

In court, no one expects the observer to learn more about the facts to which he or she testifies; no one expects the witness to give fresh testimony once the case is closed. The case of Jesus Christ is far from closed; the evidence his followers offer still mounts.

No one expects perfect holiness of the newly confirmed. Nonetheless, each of us is called to be wholly faithful, wholly good. "Be perfect, therefore, as your heavenly Father is perfect," Jesus told the throng assembled on the mountainside (Matthew 5:48).

"Perfect" holiness comes slowly. A rare child shows sanctity early. But most children, like their parents before them, ripen slowly. Virtue develops over a lifetime, the end product of lifelong faith.

Gifts of the Spirit

We speak of the "gifts of the Spirit": wisdom, understanding, counsel, fortitude, knowledge, piety and fear of the Lord. Your child will not, of course, display extraordinary knowledge or wisdom immediately after Confirmation. We do not receive these gifts in full bloom, but must nurture them over a lifetime.

The Confirmation candidate still stands at the beginning of life's journey. Years of learning, growth and deepening insight into ancient truths, years of experience with the living Lord and his people still lie ahead. The Spirit of God impels believers to witness not only to what they learned in a few months or a few years of instruction, but to what they continue to learn in shared worship and shared searching.

The faith you professed for your child at Baptism will more and more belong to a person capable of claiming the heritage and bearing witness to what life and loving people have taught—all in the Spirit of God. Now you set out together on a new journey. Great discoveries still lie ahead of you both. And the person for whom you once spoke belief may now, in the power of the Spirit, enrich your own journey in faith.

For Reflection and Discussion

- *How has your faith deepened since your own Confirmation? How have you learned more about your faith?*

- *Whose witness, spoken or lived, has most profoundly shaped your own belief?*

- *Who has been most profoundly affected by your witness, spoken or lived?*

- *Do you know who your youngster's heroes in faith are? What kind of witness have they offered?*

- *What effect has rearing this child had on your belief? Do you think this young person can contribute still more insights into your faith?*

Confirm, O God,
   what you have brought about in us,
   and preserve in the hearts of your faithful
   the gifts of the Holy Spirit:
   may they never be ashamed
   to confess Christ crucified before the world
   and by devoted charity
   may they ever fulfill his commands.

Who lives and reigns for ever and ever.
   (*The Order of Confirmation*, #33)

While staying with them, he ordered them not to leave Jerusalem, but to wait there for the promise of the Father. "This," he said, "is what you have heard from me; for John baptized with water, but you will be baptized with the Holy Spirit not many days from now.... But you will receive power when the Holy Spirit has come upon you; and you will be my witnesses in Jerusalem, in all Judea and Samaria, and to the ends of the earth." (Acts of the Apostles 1:45, 8)

In order that the message of salvation can show the power of its truth and radiance..., it must be authenticated by the witness of the life of Christians. "The witness of a Christian life and good works done in a supernatural spirit have great power to draw men to the faith and to God." (*Catechism of the Catholic Church*, #2044)

Celebrating Christian Identity: The Order of Confirmation

A cross traced in oil on the forehead and a few words ("Be sealed with the gift of the Holy Spirit") confer Confirmation. But the sacrament's full meaning rests not only in a moment's happenings, but also in the people involved and the relationships they embody.

The first person on the scene is, of course, the Confirmation candidate, your youngster. This whole book has focused on that young person, and on how the Christian identity you claimed for a newly baptized baby has become your child's own.

Human identity normally finds expression in a name. To speak of Christian identity is to add a name—*Christian, Catholic*—to the deeply personal name you spoke at Baptism. Now, at Confirmation, your child chooses that most intimate identity: a name.

Rechoosing the baptismal name as a Confirmation name is one way to affirm the birthright identity and emphasize the link with Baptism. Choosing a new name pays homage to someone (historic figure or everyday intimate) whose witness has made a real difference to a youngster. Either choice is significant.

Neither choice is *yours*. All you can do is to ask the right questions: Why this name? What does this name have to do with your child's Christian identity?

The second person on the scene is the Confirmation sponsor. In the infant Church, sponsors testified to an aspiring Christian's real interest in the new faith, to the convert's willingness to take on a dangerous and "subversive" way of life. The faith community had to trust sponsors' judgment, for the newcomer might well be an infiltrator eager to see the whole group thrown to the lions.

Ancient Gesture

Laying one's hand on an individual is an ancient biblical gesture that invokes the Spirit of God. In the celebration of Confirmation, the bishop or his delegate extends his hands over the candidates' heads before anointing them with chrism. The bishop then confers Confirmation by the laying on of the hand—anointing with chrism the forehead of the candidate—and through the words, "Be sealed with the gift of the Holy Spirit." During the anointing, the sponsor places a hand on the candidate's shoulder as a sign of support and solidarity and gives the candidate's name to the bishop (or the candidate may give her own name). After anointing, in some dioceses, the bishop may shake the hand of the candidate. Eliminated in the current rite is the blow or slap on the cheek from former rites.

You chose baptismal sponsors—godparents—without feeling such a threat. You chose them because they were models of the faith you wished to share with your child, because their love made a difference in your life.

The choice of a Confirmation sponsor is your youngster's. You can help by providing good criteria. A godparent who has been a real model of faith to your child logically completes the baptismal role by becoming a Confirmation sponsor. The Church therefore urges that a godparent serve in this role. But someone else—someone who has impressed your youngster's faith more deeply—may be your child's choice.

The final (or perhaps the first!) character in the sacramental drama is your bishop. Whether he or his delegate presides at the ceremony, the ancient prerogative of "confirming" the baptism of a child still belongs to him.

That's less a question of authority than a matter of reality. However intimate the believing community (and the family is the "domestic Church"), however personal the experience of the Lord's presence in an individual life, Catholic Christianity has a larger dimension. We trace our heritage—our identity—to the apostles who awaited the Spirit in the Upper Room. We trace our apostolic heritage through our pope and our bishops.

Confirmation is never just a parish event. The sweet-smelling oil—the chrism which consecrates your youngster in the Spirit of Christ—was blessed during Holy Week at your bishop's church, your diocesan cathedral.

Furthermore, your child's Confirmation has global significance: This child is confirmed to bear witness to the world. The relationship between what transpires in church and the waiting world is expressed in the gesture the bishop makes after the anointing: a Sign of Peace. Today's faith-family lives in a world sick with war; today's believers celebrate the vision of Christ's kingdom and share with one another the peace they are to carry beyond the church doors.

In Confirmation, your child is claimed in faith by a Church that stretches from your hometown to Rome to the most distant reaches of the planet. In Confirmation, your child is signed with the Spirit who knows no boundaries of time or space, only the possibilities of faith.

Your youngster, sealed in faith by the Spirit of God, becomes more fully what you asked on the baptismal day: a new creation in Christ, blessed with a magnificent though yet unseen future.

Notes

CPSIA information can be obtained
at www.ICGtesting.com
Printed in the USA
LVOW03s0745140218
566488LV00001B/1/P